Joy

TO THE WORLD

25 CHRISTMAS CAROL MEDITATIONS

J.JOHN

British Library Cataloguing in Publication Data
A catalogue record for this book is available from the British Library

ISBN: 978-1-912326-19-8

Scripture quotations are taken from the Holy Bible, New International Version (Anglicised
edition). Copyright © 1979, 1984, 2011 by Biblica, formerly International Bible Society.
Used by permission of Hodder & Stoughton Publishers, an Hachette UK company.
All rights reserved.

Scripture quotations marked 'New Living Translation' are taken from the Holy Bible, New
Living Translation. Copyright © 1996, 2004, 2007, 2013 by Tyndale House Foundation.
Used by permission of Tyndale House Publishers, Inc., Wheaton, Illinois 60188.
All rights reserved.

Cover design by Jonathan West, layout design by Rachel Fung

Print Management by Verité CM Ltd
www.veritecm.com

Contents

Day 1
CHRISTMAS IS ABOUT CHRIST

In this December run-up to Christmas, the nativity of Jesus Christ, I want to explore Christmas by focusing on carols and what they say. Most of the carols will be familiar to you, particularly if you've been a churchgoer for some years. Others are new. Whether they are old or new I want to use them to point to the truth of the Christmas season.

I think that doing this is helpful because the idea of *thinking* about what the carols say may strike you as a bit of a novelty.

I like carols. Musically, a lot of them are memorable. Most carols sound like dance tunes and that gives them a creative rhythm and life. Another factor is that because carols are used for only a month or so each year, they remain fresh.

In terms of what carols teach, one of the most fascinating things about these Christmas songs is that they go back centuries. Many of them were written in times and places very different from our own, and those who wrote them responded to Christmas in a way that differs from the way that we do. The result is that although they may be centuries old, there is a refreshing originality to them that can make us see Christian truth from a very different perspective.

Let me offer two reminders at the beginning of our journey through carols.

The first reminder is that Christmas is about Christ. This may seem obvious, but the fact that it is about Jesus Christ needs to be emphasised because increasingly today we are seeing a bizarre phenomenon: the focus of Christmas has come to be Christmas itself. The traditional heart of Christmas – the celebration of the coming of God into the world in Jesus – has been removed, producing a season without a reason. The modern festival of Christmas has come to focus on memories of the past, on parties, on eating and on presents. Christmas is now about Christmas. My first reminder is this: whether you celebrate Christmas loudly or quietly this December, make sure that Christ is at the centre of it.

The second reminder is that Christmas should generate joy. All too often Christmas is a draining experience and generates exhaustion or even just indifference. The modern Christmas makes an easy target for the cynic. Yet whenever the Bible talks about Christ's coming into the world, it sounds a note of *joy*. This is captured perfectly by one of the great Christmas carols 'Joy to the world'. It was written by the hymn writer Isaac Watts nearly 300 years ago. Listen to the first verse.

> Joy to the world! The Lord is come;
> Let earth receive her King;
> Let every heart prepare him room,
> And heaven and nature sing,
> And heaven and nature sing,
> And heaven, and heaven, and nature sing.

To understand Christmas is to experience joy.

Joy to the world!

Joy to the world!
The Lord is come;
Let earth receive her King;
Let every heart prepare him room,
And heaven and nature sing,
And heaven and nature sing,
And heaven, and heaven,
and nature sing.

Joy to the earth!
The Saviour reigns;
Let men their songs employ;
While fields and floods,
rocks, hills, and plains
Repeat the sounding joy,
Repeat the sounding joy,
Repeat, repeat the sounding joy.

No more let sins
and sorrows grow,
Nor thorns infest the ground;
He comes to make his blessings flow
Far as the curse is found,
Far as the curse is found,
Far as, far as,
the curse is found.

He rules the world
with truth and grace,
And makes the nations prove
The glories of his righteousness,
And wonders of his love,
And wonders of his love,
And wonders,
wonders, of his love.

Day 2
THE REASON FOR THE SEASON

We live in a peculiar age. Our technological world depends on logic, reason and science, yet increasingly we find ourselves doing things that are illogical, acting on impulse, flying in the face of reason. Films skate swiftly over gaping holes in the plot, advertisements flaunt reality, politicians appeal to sentiment rather than sense. Don't worry about the facts, just enjoy the experience!

Christmas can be a bit like that. The nativity play begins and Joseph, Mary (and, in big budget productions, the donkey) tread on to the stage. It's Christmas again! Yet we need to ask, what's actually going on? Why is the birth of Jesus 'good news'? Why are there angels? Why did the shepherds come? Perhaps, above all, the question: what's this baby doing in the manger? Why is everybody treating him as if he is God?

The important point – and it bears repeating – is that there is a *logic* to Christmas. Consider the centuries-old carol that begins 'On Christmas night all Christians sing to hear the news the angels bring; news of great joy, news of great mirth, news of our merciful King's birth'. Note that repeated reference to *joy* that I mentioned yesterday. Now listen to the second verse.

> Then why should we on earth be sad,
> Since our Redeemer made us glad?
> Then why should we on earth be sad,
> Since our Redeemer made us glad,
> When from our sin he set us free,
> All for to gain our liberty?

The long-forgotten writer of this carol says there is a reason why we should be joyful and full of mirth or happiness. There is a Redeemer: he has made us glad, because he set us free and has given us liberty. When we come across verses like this it is always worthwhile asking ourselves, 'What's going on here?' To understand this we need to go back a bit.

We do ourselves a disservice by splitting our Bibles into Old and New Testaments. Our New Testament is the fulfilment – the completion – of the Old Testament. The Old Testament is a long, winding story of how God began to deal with the mess that humankind has become. We read how, in the beginning, the human race rejected God and, in an attempt to be free, rebelled against him. In a pattern that has been repeated in an infinite number of ways since, the freedom that was sought turned out to be, in reality, slavery of the worst sort. Cut loose from a once-perfect relationship with God, the human race descended into every kind of wickedness. Human beings then and now have become slaves to our own desires and to evil itself.

The image of us being enslaved, trapped and even held hostage by evil recurs throughout the Bible. It's also something that we are all familiar with. If we have any sense we don't just see it in spectacular headline-making outbursts of violence by thuggish criminals; we see it quietly, persistently and permanently in our own lives. Despite our best efforts, we all fail to do what we know is right.

One of the terrible things about being enslaved is that we cannot free ourselves because we have no resources to do it. Someone else has to rescue us: a someone else we call a *Redeemer*. But if all the human race is enslaved, who can redeem us? The obvious answer is that if we can't redeem ourselves then only someone from outside, someone who is not themselves enslaved, can bring redemption. That someone, the New Testament tells us, is Jesus Christ, and his coming to earth as a baby marks the long, eagerly awaited arrival of the Redeemer.

There are many New Testament verses that talk about this. For example, Paul writes, 'For he [God] has rescued us from the dominion of darkness and brought us into the kingdom of the Son he loves, in whom we have redemption, the forgiveness of sins' (Colossians 1:13–14).

Christmas is about being set free from all that is wrong and that binds us and enslaves us. It is about the arrival of a liberator: a Redeemer. It's no wonder that, in the words of the carol, we can be *glad*.

On Christmas night all Christians sing

(Sussex Carol)

On Christmas night all Christians sing
To hear the news the angels bring;
On Christmas night all Christians sing
To hear the news the angels bring:
News of great joy, news of great mirth,
News of our merciful King's birth.

Then why should we on earth be sad,
Since our Redeemer made us glad?
Then why should we on earth be sad,
Since our Redeemer made us glad,
When from our sin he set us free,
All for to gain our liberty?

When sin departs before his grace,
Then life and health come in its place.
When sin departs before his grace,
Then life and health come in its place.
Angels and men with joy may sing
All for to see the new-born King.

All out of darkness we have light,
Which made the angels sing this night;
All out of darkness we have light,
Which made the angels sing this night:
'Glory to God and peace to men,
Now and forevermore. Amen.'

Day 3
CHRISTMAS IS ABOUT DELIVERANCE FROM EVIL

At this time of year it's quite common to hear some weary adult, probably suffering from Pre-Christmas Stress Disorder, say, 'Of course, Christmas is just for children.' Actually, they couldn't be more wrong. There are deep aspects to Christmas and some of them are very adult. A repeated idea in Christmas carols is that we are enslaved to evil and we need to have redemption. A Redeemer needs to step in and save us and that Redeemer is Jesus.

Actually, a number of carols point out a deeper and darker truth. It is not just that we are enslaved to some abstract principle of evil; we are enslaved to the evil *one*. Now if we are to have anything like an authentic view of what this season of Christ's nativity is ultimately all about, there are three truths here which we cannot omit.

The first truth is quite simply that there is more to this world than we can see, touch or measure in a laboratory. Although the word is misused and ridiculed, we need to acknowledge the existence of the *supernatural*. We can try and remove the supernatural from the nativity story but we are not left with much other than 'child of unmarried mother born in miserable circumstances'. I don't know about you, but I can't get excited about that.

The reality is that most of the world, most of the time, has believed in a supernatural of some sort. Of course, truth is not some sort of democratic process decided by what view gets the most votes, but it's worth bearing in mind. In fact, we need an awful lot of faith to deny the supernatural, particularly when we read of some of the things theoretical physicists talk about: for example, it is generally held that they have no idea what 85 per cent of the mass of the universe actually is. That's a significant failure in the area of cosmic accountancy and, until it's remedied, I'm quite happy to believe in the supernatural world.

The second truth is that there is an *evil* supernatural. It's a recurrent point in the Bible that there are good supernatural powers under God, and bad supernatural powers under the devil or Satan. While it may be fashionable to dismiss Satan, if you look at the news there is substantial evidence for his activity.

The third truth is that as a result of our rebellion from God, human beings have found themselves on the wrong side of the supernatural. We need to be liberated and redeemed – not simply from some impersonal force of evil but from 'the Evil One'. In one of the letters of the New Testament, we read this statement about Christ's coming: 'The reason the Son of God appeared was to destroy the devil's work' (1 John 3:8). Another writer says this of Jesus: 'Since the children have flesh and blood, he too shared in their humanity so that by his death he might break the power of him who holds the power of death – that is, the devil' (Hebrews 2:14).

The heartening and reassuring idea of a Redeemer who has come to break the power of the evil one who enslaves the world is found in many Christmas carols. It's in one of the oldest Christmas carols, 'God rest you merry, gentlemen'. (Incidentally, do notice that there is a comma between merry and gentlemen.) It's the idea that because Christ has come we should no longer be dismayed but be happy and cheerful because Jesus Christ our Saviour has come to save us from the power of Satan.

> God rest you merry, gentlemen,
> Let nothing you dismay,
> For Jesus Christ, our Saviour
> Was born upon this day,
> To save us all from Satan's power
> When we were gone astray.

It may be that for you the idea of there being evil power in the universe is purely theoretical. But it may be that you are conscious of a real evil presence in your life. If that is so, then I advise you to pray the Lord's Prayer daily (Matthew 6:9–13). We need to remember at Christmas that the Redeemer has come and the power of the devil has been broken.

God rest you merry, gentlemen

God rest you merry, gentlemen,
Let nothing you dismay,
For Jesus Christ, our Saviour
Was born upon this day,
To save us all from Satan's power
When we were gone astray.
O tidings of comfort and joy,
comfort and joy,
O tidings of comfort and joy!

In Bethlehem in Jewry,
This blessed Babe was born,
And laid within a manger,
Upon this blessed morn;
The which his mother Mary
Nothing did take in scorn.
O tidings . . .

From God our heavenly Father,
A blessed angel came,
And unto certain shepherds,
Brought tidings of the same,
How that in Bethlehem was born,
The Son of God by name.
O tidings . . .

The shepherds at those tidings,
Rejoiced much in mind,
And left their flocks a-feeding,
In tempest, storm and wind,
And went to Bethlehem straightway,
This blessed babe to find.
O tidings . . .

But when to Bethlehem they came,
Whereat this Infant lay,
They found him in a manger,
Where oxen feed on hay;
His mother Mary kneeling,
Unto the Lord did pray.
O tidings . . .

Now to the Lord sing praises,
All you within this place,
And with true love and brotherhood,
Each other now embrace.
The holy tide of Christmas
All other doth efface.
O tidings . . .

Day 4
CHRISTMAS IS PART OF GOD'S BIG STORY: 1

Once upon a time, the story of the Bible was really well known. After all, for many people it was the only book they had. And in a time before a hundred channels of high-definition satellite TV, unlimited internet sites and a zillion computer games, people read it for pleasure. The result of this is that carol writers could, and did, make references to all sorts of things that now have us wondering!

Think, for instance, of one of our oldest Christmas hymns, 'O come, O come, Emmanuel', which may well be 900 years old. Let's look at the first verse alone:

O come, O come, Emmanuel,
And ransom captive Israel,
That mourns in lonely exile here,
Until the Son of God appear.
Rejoice! Rejoice! Emmanuel
Shall come to thee, O Israel.

A not unreasonable sequence of questions would include, 'Who is Emmanuel?', 'Why is he going to ransom captive Israel?' And why are they mourning 'in lonely exile here'? And that's just the first verse.

First, let's think briefly about *Emmanuel*, a name that appears in a number of carols. It is a title used in a very significant prophecy in Isaiah and it means 'God with us'. Given that most of our problems come from our separation from God, the idea that the coming deliverer will allow God to be with us is the very richest of promises.

But what about the exile and captivity bit? A central Bible narrative is about how the human race rebelled against God and became enslaved to evil. But, in his mercy, God chose to rescue the human race and began by choosing one man, Abraham, and from him and his descendants created a special people, the Jews. Over 2,000 years God communicated with his people – who had come to be called Israel – through teaching, prophecies and discipline. The relationship between God and his people was for the most part strained but, briefly, the people obeyed and God blessed them. At the time of King David and his son King Solomon, God's people lived God's way in God's land. These were, if you like, the glory days.

But the glory days were only a few decades. The rot set in. Once more, God's people disobeyed him and some six centuries before the birth of Jesus, Israel was taken into captivity in Babylon. Although around seventy years later God's people were released and returned back to the Promised Land, the good old days never returned. At the time of Jesus' birth five centuries later, God's people still felt they were in captivity and mourning 'in lonely exile' here. Like any hostage, they desperately needed someone to come and ransom them. They looked forward to the Redeemer who would ransom them, the one whom they called the Messiah or, to use the Greek, the *Christ*.

So what does this mean to us? The major point is that we should rejoice because God has kept his promises to his people. It's an encouragement to us to hang on in there with God – he may take his time but he will deliver. He has always done so in the past and he will do so in the future.

O come, O come, Emmanuel

O come, O come, Emmanuel,
And ransom captive Israel,
That mourns in lonely exile here,
Until the Son of God appear
Rejoice! Rejoice! Emmanuel
Shall come to thee, O Israel.

O come, thou Rod of Jesse, free
Thine own from Satan's tyranny;
From depths of hell thy people save,
And give them victory o'er the grave.
Rejoice! Rejoice! Emmanuel
Shall come to thee, O Israel.

O come, thou Dayspring, from on high,
And cheer us by thy drawing nigh;
Disperse the gloomy clouds of night,
And death's dark shadows put to flight.
Rejoice! Rejoice! Emmanuel
Shall come to thee, O Israel.

O come, thou Key of David, come
And open wide our heavenly home;
Make safe the way that leads on high,
And close the path to misery
Rejoice! Rejoice! Emmanuel
Shall come to thee, O Israel.

O come, Adonai, Lord of might,
Who to thy tribes, on Sinai's height,
In ancient times didst give the law
In cloud and majesty and awe
Rejoice! Rejoice! Emmanuel
Shall come to thee, O Israel.

Day 5
CHRISTMAS IS PART OF GOD'S BIG STORY: 2

Let us look at a passage from one of the most well known of all carols, 'While shepherds watched their flocks by night'.

> To you in David's town this day
> Is born of David's line
> A Saviour who is Christ the Lord,
> And this shall be the sign.

There seems to be some sort of universal human belief that somewhere in the past there was a point where our country, our world, or we took the wrong direction. For Jewish people at the time of Jesus' birth, the point where it all went wrong was well known. It was just after the reign of King David, the second king of Israel who brought peace and stability. After David came his son Solomon and although there was much about Solomon's reign that was good, he didn't just sow the seeds of the future tragedy but watered them. From then on it was downhill from decay into disaster. And at the time of Jesus' birth it's a sad but revealing fact that even though the golden days of King David's reign were a thousand years ago, it's what everybody looked back to.

Yet it wasn't simply nostalgia. Against all the odds, there was hope. The reason for the hope was quite simply the fact that the Jewish people believed that God – the Lord of history, the one who had founded their nation – had made a promise, a *covenant*, that David's line would continue. So there was the faith that one day there would be a new Messiah, from the line of David, who would put everything to rights. This new Messiah, the *Christ*, would defeat all the enemies of Israel, including the Roman occupiers, get rid of all who were opposed to the true faith and rule with justice. One day the Messiah would arrive and the new glorious rule of God would begin again.

David's birthplace was Bethlehem and there was a widespread belief based on a verse in the book of Micah that the new King would be born there. So you can understand something of the significance in the Bible and in the carols of this baby being born from the line of David and in Bethlehem. Both Matthew and Luke in their gospels make the point that Jesus was a descendant of David. Both Mary and Joseph, who in effect legally adopted Jesus, were of the royal line. For those who saw what was happening that first Christmas there was the glimmer of hope that the long-delayed liberating Messiah had, at last, arrived.

Actually it isn't just the Jewish people at the time of the birth of Christ who looked back at the turning point where history went wrong. Many of us – perhaps most of us, particularly as we get older – find ourselves looking back with regret. We look back to some turning point in our life with a sense of disappointment. There, we say, is where it all went wrong. It was there that I made the wrong choice of friends; there I made a bad decision.

Yet the fact is that Christmas is *good* news. In the northern hemisphere it is just a couple of days after the shortest day; it's the point when the world itself is actually turning around. Christmas is all about a God who keeps his promises to his people. It's a reminder that if we have put our faith in Christ we trust him for healing and restoration. With Christ a bad past can be turned into a good future. In this life, that healing may only be partial; some things that are done cannot be undone this side of eternity. But we are assured that there will be a time when everything will be made new and good and right. And that's a very important part of the good news of Christmas.

While shepherds watched

While shepherds watched their flocks by night
All seated on the ground
The angel of the Lord came down
And glory shone around.

'Fear not,' said he, for mighty dread
Had seized their troubled mind;
'Glad tidings of great joy I bring
To you and all mankind.

'To you in David's town this day
Is born of David's line
A Saviour who is Christ the Lord,
And this shall be the sign:

'The heavenly Babe you there shall find
To human view displayed,
All meanly wrapped in swaddling bands
And in a manger laid.'

Thus spake the seraph, and forthwith
Appeared a shining throng
Of angels praising God, who thus
Addressed their joyful song:

'All glory be to God on high
And on the earth be peace.
Goodwill henceforth from heaven to men
Begin and never cease!'

Day 6
MARY AND THE ANNUNCIATION

Many carols talk of Mary, one of which is 'The angel Gabriel from heaven came'. The second verse goes like this:

'For know a blessed mother thou shalt be,
All generations laud and honour thee,
Thy Son shall be Emmanuel, by seers foretold
Most highly favoured lady,' Gloria!

Actually, from the human side of things it's with Mary that the story begins. In Luke Chapter 1, Mary is told by the angel Gabriel that she is going to conceive and give birth to a son who will be called Jesus, who is going to be the long-hoped-for King and deliverer. If you know the story you know that at this point Mary raises the not inconsiderable objection that she is a virgin. Gabriel, however, responds that the conception will be through the Holy Spirit and quite simply that 'the power of the Most High will overshadow you'. To this Mary answers, 'I am the Lord's servant. May your word to me be fulfilled.'

What we call 'the virgin birth' but technically is 'the virgin conception', is a miracle that is unique in the Bible. There are several cases where God allows infertile couples to miraculously have a child but that is very different to this situation in which a woman conceives without the aid of a man.

Although the virgin conception of Jesus raises issues that are beyond our comprehension, there is logic to it.

The first thing that should be said is that the virgin conception is necessary because the human race's big problem, our alienation from God, is so deep-rooted that we human beings cannot solve it ourselves. *We* are the problem and because of that we cannot be the solution. To save the human race, God himself has to intervene.

The second thing that needs saying is that to save us, God must become one of us. The process of the *Incarnation* – which simply means God taking on human flesh and blood – is all about the way God has to deal with people. In the rather depressing discussions of military action in various parts of the world, it is very common to hear soldiers say that what we need in order to win is 'boots on the ground'. Behind this phrase is the idea that some battles cannot be won from a distance. The great battle in which God grapples with evil and destroys its power at the cross is exactly one of those: he has to be involved at the human level. And that means being born as one of us.

But let's have a right view of Mary. We should honour and respect her for her astonishing faith and trust. It's worth reminding ourselves that the visit of the angel could not have been entirely welcome to someone who was probably in her teens. Mary would have been all too aware of how her culture viewed pregnancy outside marriage and what it would mean in terms of wagging tongues, nasty accusations and even physical threats. What was to become good news for us wasn't going to be good news for her.

In agreeing to give birth to the Messiah, Mary sets the deepest example to us of obedience. It's easy to say that she showed *humility*, but what we see with Mary, particularly in her song of rejoicing that the church has come to call the *Magnificat*, is something far rarer and far greater: a cheerful, even joyful acceptance of God's will.

'I am the Lord's servant.' Is that something we can say?

The angel Gabriel from heaven came

(Gabriel's Message)

The angel Gabriel from heaven came
His wings as drifted snow, his eyes as flame
'All hail,' said he, 'thou lowly maiden Mary,
Most highly favoured lady,' Gloria!

'For know a blessed mother thou shalt be,
All generations laud and honour thee,
Thy Son shall be Emmanuel, by seers foretold,
Most highly favoured lady,' Gloria!

Then gentle Mary meekly bowed her head,
'To me be as it pleaseth God,' she said,
'My soul shall laud and magnify his holy name.'
Most highly favoured lady. Gloria!

Of her, Emmanuel, the Christ was born
In Bethlehem, all on a Christmas morn,
And Christian folk throughout the world will ever say:
'Most highly favoured lady,' Gloria!

Day 7
THE BIRTH OF CHRIST AS A HISTORICAL EVENT

Star Wars: The Force Awakens, a film set, like its predecessors, 'A long time ago in a galaxy far, far away . . .' When we think about Christmas one of the dangers we face is of imagining that the story of the nativity belongs in another unreal universe.

Part of the problem is children's nativity plays themselves. I'm a great fan of them and respect anybody who puts one on in this era of political correctness when the expectation is to produce tales of multiculturalism, social inclusion and gender fluidity. The peril with them, however, is that we can come to believe that the events of the first Christmas belong in some child's fantasy like the *Wizard of Oz*. There is a real danger that we begin to think of the Bethlehem of the nativity as if it existed in Middle Earth or

Narnia. This sort of perception is encouraged by the annual Christmas pantomime. The threat of confusion is obvious: there seems to be a risk of 'Snow White and the Seven Shepherds', 'The Three Wise Bears' or even 'Cinderella and the Angels'. Of course, we also mustn't forget the efforts of those noisy atheists or sceptical theologians who think that the biblical accounts belong in the realm of make-believe.

Yet to read the accounts in Matthew and Luke of the birth of Jesus is to be reminded that they were written as history, not fantasy. Luke gives a very specific time reference involving emperors and governments. Although we may struggle with precisely identifying it, it is clear that he is claiming to write about a historical event that actually happened. In Matthew, history intrudes with the very real and very unpleasant Herod the Great. That concern for history runs throughout the New Testament and continues into the early church. So, for example, the Apostles' Creed mentions that Jesus 'was conceived by the Holy Spirit, born of the Virgin Mary, suffered under Pontius Pilate'. Here we have the miraculous conception linked with someone known to history, a governor of the Roman province of Judaea from AD 26 to 36 and a man noted for governing with the unfortunate qualities of insensitivity, brutality and incompetence. Pilate is also mentioned in the creed not to be blamed but to remind Christians that their faith is anchored on what actually happened.

The reality of the first Christmas also has a real geography: Jerusalem, Bethlehem, Nazareth are all real places and regularly feature in the news today, if, sadly, often for the wrong reasons. The politics are real too. We see a near-bankrupt Roman Empire with an emperor who is desperately trying to find ways of raising revenue; that empire's thuggish and corrupt forces of occupation; and its puppet king, increasingly paranoid in his old age. It's all too real.

Songs of any kind often fight shy of reality. Yet interestingly, a number of carols make specific reference to the historical situation. Take, for instance, 'A virgin most pure', which is nearly 400 years old. In its second verse we sing:

At Bethlehem city, in Jewry it was
Where Joseph and Mary together did pass,
And there to be taxed, with many one more,
For Caesar commanded the same should be so.

Here, in the middle of a carol about the coming of God to the human race in Christ, we get a reference to Roman tax policy. When we sing carols or hear the Christmas story, we need to remember that this is not some imagined fantastic legend but an account set in a real world in a real place with real people. And that, of course, gives it its truthful importance. If the first Christmas were fictional, it could be considered interesting and slightly charming but ultimately no more relevant to how we live than one of the myths about Hercules or the tale of Cinderella. If it is true, however, then it has extraordinary relevance. Christmas presents us with a challenge. If it is true, and if somehow in this infant God *was* breaking into our world, then it is quite simply the most important event in the history of our planet. And it is something we need to do something about.

A virgin most pure

A virgin most pure, as the prophets do tell,
Hath brought forth a baby, as it hath befell,
To be our Redeemer from death, hell and sin,
Which Adam's transgression has wrappèd us in.

Refrain:
And therefore be merry, set sorrow aside;
Christ Jesus our Saviour was born on this tide.

At Bethlehem city, in Jewry it was
Where Joseph and Mary together did pass,
And there to be taxed, with many one more,
For Caesar commanded the same should be so. *Refrain*

But, when they had entered the city so fair
A number of people so mighty was there,
That Joseph and Mary, whose substance was small,
Could get in the city no lodging at all. *Refrain*

Then were they constrained in a stable to lie,
Where oxen and asses they used for to tie;
Their lodging so simple, they held it no scorn,
But against the next morning our Saviour was born. *Refrain*

The King of all glory to this world being brought,
Small store of fine linen to wrap him was sought,
When Mary had swaddled her young Son so sweet,
Within an ox manger she laid him to sleep. *Refrain*

Then God sent an angel from heaven so high,
To certain poor shepherds in fields where they lie,
And bade them no longer in sorrow to stay,
Because that our Saviour was born on this day. *Refrain*

Then presently after, the shepherds did spy
A number of angels appear in the sky;
Who joyfully talked and sweetly did sing,
To God be all glory, our heavenly King. *Refrain*

Day 8
THE NATURE OF THE INCARNATION AND ITS MEANING FOR THE WORLD

Most of us will at some time have enjoyed the spicy delight of chilli con carne. Many of us will know that it literally means 'chilli with meat'. That little Spanish word *carne* goes back to the Latin which surfaces in the English word *Incarnation*. That's a word Christians use when we talk about the first Christmas: the awesome, mind-blowing idea that in Jesus, God was taking on human flesh.

From the earliest days, the Christian church held out that Jesus of Nazareth was not simply man but someone who was also

God. Exactly what that meant was the subject of a long series of church councils over hundreds of years, in which some of the finest minds of the age debated the issue, sometimes with far more heat than light. The conclusion was that somehow, in a manner beyond precise definition, Jesus had the properties of both man and God. I don't think we should get too worried that no one has come up with a precise explanation of how it works. After all, we cannot fully understand God our Creator because he is infinitely superior in every way to us.

Almost all carols mention the Incarnation, most expressing wonder that somehow God would condescend to become one of us.

Actually, the fact that the first followers of Jesus concluded that he could be worshipped as God is remarkable. The first Christians were Jews and the Jewish religion, then as now, was committed to the belief that there is only one God. At the central part of Jewish daily worship is this phrase: 'Hear, O Israel: the LORD our God, the LORD is one.' It is a permanent reminder of the hard-learned truth that there is just one God and that he does not share that position with anybody or anything. The extraordinary thing is that after Jesus' death and resurrection, his followers began to talk about him using language that was normally reserved only for God. Indeed, they worshipped him *as* God.

The Incarnation, however, is not simply a hypothetical puzzle to do with the exact nature of Jesus' identity. It is astonishingly relevant.

It is relevant to who Jesus *is*. Jesus is a mediator: someone who is a go-between. And the best mediators are those who have a foot in both camps: they speak both languages, have dual nationality, and understand both parties. Jesus is the perfect mediator between God and humankind because he is both God and human.

It is relevant to what Jesus *did*. At the heart of Christianity is the truth that Jesus died for his followers. Now, if he was just a man – even a perfect man – that truth makes no logical sense. One human being, even a perfect one, can only die for another human being. If, however, Jesus was not just man but also the infinite God then his death becomes much more significant: he can die for an infinite number of people. For you, for me, for anybody else who surrender's to him.

It is relevant to who he is *now*. Jesus has ascended into heaven, where we can pray to him. If he was just a man it's difficult to see how that works – after all, that particular prayer channel gets a lot of traffic. But if Jesus is God he can handle the prayers of millions. Equally, as man, Jesus can sympathise with our needs and problems; as God he has the power to answer them.

The truth that the infant cradled in the manger is in fact God is widespread throughout carols. Take, for instance, the very well-known 'Away in a manger' with the phrase 'The little Lord Jesus laid down his sweet head'. The word *Lord* there is a title for God. The infant asleep in the cattle trough is the maker of the universe. That is the most staggering, life-changing truth ever proclaimed. Christmas challenges us to decide.

Away in a manger

Away in a manger, no crib for his bed,
The little Lord Jesus laid down his sweet head.
The stars in the bright sky looked down where he lay,
The little Lord Jesus asleep on the hay.

The cattle are lowing, the baby awakes.
But little Lord Jesus, no crying he makes.
I love thee, Lord Jesus, look down from the sky,
And stay by my side until morning is nigh.

Be near me, Lord Jesus, I ask thee to stay
Close by me for ever, and love me, I pray.
Bless all the dear children in thy tender care,
And take us to heaven, to live with thee there.

Day 9
THE MEANING OF THE INCARNATION FOR US

The Incarnation: the extraordinary, mind-boggling way in which God became one of us in Jesus. There is an awesome mystery in how God becomes flesh. It is incomprehensible but not illogical.

Christmas carols celebrate this truth. Take, for instance, 'O come, all ye faithful'. The second verse goes as follows:

> God of God,
> Light of Light,
> Lo, he abhors not the virgin's womb;
> Very God,

Begotten, not created:
O come, let us adore him,
Christ the Lord.

There are some powerful insights wrapped up in language that we probably would not use ourselves today. What is being said here – and it's largely taken from one of the great creeds of the church[1] – is something along the following lines. First, the utterly perfect God – he who was 'Light of Light' – was prepared to accept being confined in the darkness of Mary's womb. Second, the infant Jesus is not *something* created by God but *someone* who actually *is* God. And thirdly, the carol encourages us to adore Jesus as God.

The Incarnation is so important that it changes almost everything. Let me draw your attention to two specific issues.

The Incarnation tells us that history has a purpose. The 18th-century historian Edward Gibbon wrote cynically that 'History is indeed little more than the register of crimes, follies, and misfortunes of humankind.' Yet if God chose to become a member of the human race then that shows his commitment to us and our world. We may not understand where history is going but if we believe in the Incarnation we can be assured it is in safe hands. The fact that God loved this world so much that he became one of us is a guarantee that our world has a future.

The Incarnation tells us that human beings have dignity and value. Our modern way of thinking has greatly distorted how we human beings think of ourselves. Once upon a time human beings considered themselves to be utterly unique and above everything else. We were made in the image of God and just a little lower than the angels. Such a view had its problems and was abused, but we knew who we were. Today we hear from those who understand biology that we are no more than animals. We hear from those inspired by technology, that much of what makes us special is either already, or soon will be, duplicated by computers. The combination of both views produces the conclusion that the human race is merely a temporary interlude between a world dominated by animals and one governed by robots.

On a practical level, business and industry view us simply as 'consumers' or 'purchasers'. Politicians see us as no more than 'the electorate'. Everywhere there are bureaucracies that treat us as no more than digits on a spreadsheet. You don't have to be paranoid to worry that, in the modern world, human beings are becoming disposable items.

The Incarnation stands utterly against this depressing view. It's an old idea that, in Jesus, God descended to where we are so that we might ascend to where he is. He became a child that we might become children of God.

Take home a truth for yourself at Christmas. God is committed to this world and to you. There is a value to this world and a value to you. At the start of the Bible it says that God created human beings in his image. Yet in the nativity of Christ, God becomes one of us, and we now understand that we human beings are indeed in the image of God. To see any human being is to see something that God allowed himself to become. That truth has a meaning for everybody we are in contact with. Whoever you meet – whether they are a street cleaner or a film star, a brilliant student or a senior citizen, or someone from the other end of the world – when you look at them you see the image of God.

O come, all ye faithful

O come, all ye faithful,
Joyful and triumphant!
O come ye, O come ye to Bethlehem;
Come and behold him
Born the King of angels:

Refrain:
O come, let us adore him,
O come, let us adore him,
O come, let us adore him,
Christ the Lord.

God of God,
Light of Light,
Lo, he abhors not the virgin's womb;
Very God,
Begotten, not created: *Refrain*

Sing, choirs of angels,
Sing in exultation,
Sing, all ye citizens of heaven above!
'Glory to God
In the highest': *Refrain*

Yea, Lord, we greet thee,
Born this happy morning;
Jesus, to thee be glory given;
Word of the Father,
Now in flesh appearing: *Refrain*

Day 10
THE LOVE OF
GOD AT CHRISTMAS

As everybody knows, one of the common themes of traditional romantic fiction is the story that centres on the rich boy who meets a poor girl. He is from a privileged social background but he falls in love with a girl from the bottom of the pile. The tension is easily generated. Is it at all possible, we ask, that our hero will give up all that he has and all that he is for her? And again in the traditional stories, what happens is that our hero finds himself so deeply in love with the girl that he throws everything away for her. The amount that he gives away – whether wealth, status or career – in order to gain his loved one, tells us exactly how much he loves her.

Now of course we cannot completely equate God's love for human beings with romantic love. For one thing, in the Greek of the New Testament they are two very different words and very different concepts.

Nevertheless, this idea that the amount you love someone can be indicated by the amount you give up for them is something very relevant to the Christmas story. If we take Christian theology seriously we will realise that God did not *have* to do the 'becoming a human being' business. Our first ancestors had been warned that there would be serious consequences if they decided to break God's rules. Despite that solemn warning, they did indeed rebel. At this point God could with perfect justice have said, 'You have broken my commands. Goodbye, human race.'

Yet, instead of wiping out humanity at the start, God allowed us to continue, but in doing so began to prepare a long-term rescue programme. In what we call the Old Testament the nature of the rescue plan is slowly but progressively hinted at. We have touched already on one of the key themes: a king from the lineage of David. Yet there are other hints. So, for instance, in some of the later chapters of Isaiah there is mention of a remarkable figure, a servant, who seems to be both man and

God, who comes and suffers terribly in order to rescue God's people from their sins.

The great Christian message is that God descends from the very highest place to the very lowest place in order to rescue us. That is no fancy idea dreamed up by philosophy but is clearly taught in the New Testament. In the letter to the Philippian church, the apostle Paul writes the following:

> In your relationships with one another, have the same mind-set as Christ Jesus: who, being in very nature God, did not consider equality with God something to be used to his own advantage; rather, he made himself nothing by taking the very nature of a servant, being made in human likeness. And being found in appearance as a man, he humbled himself by becoming obedient to death – even death on a cross! (Philippians 2:5–8)

Many Christmas carols note this theme. One of the best-written Christmas carols is 'In the bleak midwinter' by the Victorian poet Christina Rossetti. It is full of a sense of awe at what God did in Christ.

If you are feeling low this Christmas, doubting the value of who you are, consider what this means. God loved you so much that he went through the inconceivable undertaking of descending down to become one of us in order to rescue you. And if you think the descent to being a baby that we celebrate at Christmas was extraordinary, wait until you get to the Easter message, of death on a cross. If that doesn't encourage you, I don't know what will.

In the bleak midwinter

In the bleak midwinter
Frosty wind made moan,
Earth stood hard as iron,
Water like a stone;
Snow had fallen, snow on snow,
Snow on snow,
In the bleak midwinter
Long ago.

Our God, heaven cannot hold him
Nor earth sustain;
Heaven and earth shall flee away
When he comes to reign:
In the bleak midwinter
A stable-place sufficed
The Lord God Almighty,
Jesus Christ.

Enough for him, whom cherubim
Worship night and day,
A breastful of milk,
And a mangerful of hay;
Enough for him, whom angels
Fall down before,
The ox and ass and camel
Which adore.

Angels and archangels
May have gathered there,
Cherubim and seraphim
Thronged the air,
But only his mother
In her maiden bliss,
Worshipped the beloved
With a kiss.

What can I give him,
Poor as I am?
If I were a shepherd
I would bring a lamb;
If I were a wise man
I would do my part;
Yet what I can, I give him,
Give my heart.

Day 11
POWER AND POWERLESSNESS

Although we may not talk much about it, from our earliest days we are always aware of who has power and who doesn't. Consider the Christmas story: it's pretty obvious who are the powerful and who are the powerless.

There are the *powerful*. Emperor Caesar Augustus runs the vast Roman Empire and controls palaces, cities and armies. He has the power of life and death over everyone and is so mighty that he can summon people fifteen hundred miles away to travel across the country to attend tax offices. There is the power of King Herod the Great, a man of wealth and with such authority that at a word he can summon the religious leaders and with a command have a village's infants slaughtered.

Then there are the *powerless*. Mary and Joseph are summoned by imperial orders to travel across their nation to register for tax. At Bethlehem their only accommodation is the most basic possible. The infant is born in the humblest possible setting, placed in a feeding trough next to the animals. Within months they will be refugees fleeing from a deadly persecution into Egypt.

And yet the Christmas story is that behind these contrasts between the powerful and the powerless there is something else. The appearance and the reality are very different. King Herod, increasingly prone to depression and paranoia, will die in misery within a year. Within seventy years his crowning achievement, the Temple, will be levelled and his entire dynasty a matter of history. Emperor Caesar Augustus will survive for another twenty years, dying at the age of seventy-five. The empire that he creates will eventually crumble to dust and ruins.

And the infant Jesus? The powerless baby? In one sense he stays powerless. Eventually, the man the baby becomes will die pinned to a cross, unable to move: the very definition of powerlessness. Yet God will raise him and he will be proclaimed as Saviour across the world. Within three centuries, Augustus' mighty empire will bow before Jesus as Lord and King. The calendars of the entire world come to be centred on that birth in Bethlehem.

Many carols highlight the awesome paradox that although the nativity of Christ is surrounded by poverty and humility, in reality things are very different. One carol that does this well is the 'Calypso Carol':

> See him lying on a bed of straw,
> Draughty stable with an open door,
> Mary cradling the babe she bore;
> The Prince of Glory is his name.

It reminds us that the babe bedded in straw is in fact the Lord of all.

The Christmas story tells us that we should not to be seduced by power. The glittering kingdoms of this world – whether based on finance or on military, political or media influence – stumble and fall with astonishing frequency and speed. Many of us spend our lives trying to scramble up the ladder of career and success in these kingdoms. Christmas reminds us that we are utterly foolish to base our lives on what the world considers to be power. Others of us find that life has treated us in such a way that we belong more with the powerless than the powerful. If this Christmas you find yourself in that situation, be encouraged! If you have put your faith in Christ then you can be confident that in the long term things will be very different.

The Christmas message also has implications for how we view others. We should constantly remind ourselves that those who consider themselves powerful are actually no more valuable than those who find themselves powerless. This Christmas let's be concerned for everyone, whether they seem to have everything or nothing. One day, here too, things will be very different.

See him lying on a bed of straw

(Calypso Carol)

See him lying on a bed of straw,
Draughty stable with an open door,
Mary cradling the babe she bore;
The Prince of Glory is his name.

Refrain:
Oh, now carry me to Bethlehem
To see the Lord appear to men;
Just as poor as was the stable then,
The prince of glory when he came.

Star of silver sweep across the skies,
Show where Jesus in the manger lies.
Shepherds swiftly from your stupor rise
To see the Saviour of the world. *Refrain*

Mine are riches from thy poverty,
From thine innocence, eternity;
Mine, forgiveness by thy death for me
Child of sorrow, for my joy. *Refrain*

Angels, sing again the song you sang,
Bring God's glory to the heart of man;
Sing how Bethlehem's little baby can
Be salvation to the soul. *Refrain*

Day 12
GOD WITH US

There are many situations in life where one of the sweetest phrases we can hear is, 'Don't worry, I'll come with you.' Whether it's as a child going to school for the first time, a visit to the hospital or just simply driving to a new address in the centre of a busy town, the idea that someone who can help is going to come with us is reassuring and encouraging.

Many Christmas carols refer to Jesus using the name *Immanuel* or *Emmanuel*. It occurs in Matthew's Gospel in his account of how Jesus came to be conceived by the Holy Spirit. There we read: 'All this took place to fulfil what the Lord had said through the prophet: "The virgin will conceive and give birth to a son, and they will call him Immanuel" (which means "God with us")' (Matthew 1:22–23).

Matthew is referring here to a prophecy in Isaiah (7:14) where there is a prediction of deliverance for God's people through a child who will be born to a woman who was a virgin. In whatever way this prediction was understood at the time it was given, Matthew sees its fulfilment in Jesus being born miraculously from the Virgin Mary.

That name *Emmanuel*, which, as Matthew purposely mentions, means 'God with us', is extraordinarily rich. It points us back to Genesis where we see not just that the human race was created to live in fellowship with God but how that fellowship was broken by our rebellion. The result of that ancient rift between God and us is that, by nature, human beings feel God is either distant or absent from them. In the Old Testament, God's people Israel felt that, as a nation, God was present with them in the Tabernacle and later the Temple. As individuals, however, they seem to have only rarely known God's presence. For all their sacrifices, prayers and praise, the God who should have been with them remained far off.

The coming of Jesus changes this. You could say that Jesus was God with us in the same sense that those who followed him around the Holy Land had God in some way living on earth among them. Yet it goes much deeper than this. By dying on the cross, Jesus paid the penalty that humankind could not pay. This cancellation of the great debt of the human race means that at last God could be present with his people and that they could know him personally.

A further development of the idea that Jesus allows God to be with his followers is the fact that, when he ascended to heaven, Jesus sent the Holy Spirit to be on earth with those who had put their trust in him. In John's Gospel, the Holy Spirit is called by a Greek word *parakletos*, which means 'someone who stands alongside another'. It can have a precise legal meaning like 'advocate for the defence' or it can just mean 'someone who comes beside to give help or support'. Those who have put their faith in Jesus receive the gift of the Holy Spirit and through him come to know God with them. The idea of Emmanuel has become a reality.

Emmanuel gets a mention in many Christmas carols, including 'Hark! the herald angels sing', which is very much a dream team product with deep and thoughtful words by Charles Wesley, the great hymn writer, tweaked by George Whitfield, the great evangelist, and with music from Felix Mendelssohn, the great composer. Here is the second verse:

> Christ, by highest heaven adored;
> Christ, the everlasting Lord;
> Late in time behold him come,
> Offspring of a virgin's womb.
> Veiled in flesh the Godhead see;
> Hail th'incarnate Deity,
> Pleased as man with us to dwell,
> Jesus, our Emmanuel.

Emmanuel 'God with us' is a tremendous truth. To know God's presence is the antidote to life's problems such as fear, suffering, loneliness. But to know God's presence in Christ through the Holy Spirit is also the secret to the contented life. Christmas is a time when we think of Jesus being born into the world and so getting alongside the human race. *True*. But Christmas is also a time when Jesus is not only born into the world but born into our lives. And this season it's wise to check whether we know Emmanuel, God with us.

Hark! the herald angels sing

Hark! the herald angels sing,
'Glory to the new born King;
Peace on earth and mercy mild,
God and sinners reconciled!'
Joyful, all ye nations rise,
Join the triumph of the skies;
With th'angelic host proclaim,
'Christ is born in Bethlehem!'

Refrain:
Hark! the herald angels sing,
'Glory to the newborn King!'

Christ, by highest heaven adored;
Christ, the everlasting Lord;
Late in time behold him come,
Offspring of a virgin's womb.
Veiled in flesh the Godhead see;
Hail th'incarnate Deity,
Pleased as man with us to dwell,
Jesus, our Emmanuel. *Refrain*

Hail the heaven-born
Prince of Peace!
Hail the Sun of Righteousness!
Light and life to all he brings,
Ris'n with healing in his wings.
Mild, he lays his glory by,
Born that we no more may die;
Born to raise us from the earth,
Born to give us second birth. *Refrain*

Day 13
HAVE A WONDER-FILLED CHRISTMAS

Is there a busier time of year than Christmas? The parties, school plays, supermarket queues, the wrapping up of presents, the posting of Christmas cards?

It's not as though the hard work ends at midnight on the 24th either. There's all the excitement on 25th December, which, as anyone with small children will know, could start at three in the morning! Then, immediately afterwards, there are the traditional post-Christmas rituals of 'Returning the Unwanted Presents' and 'Writing Thank-you Letters'. And then, suddenly, it's New Year and we're back to work. Christmas can leave us tired for all the wrong reasons.

Even Christmas services seem to suffer from a seasonal busyness. There has to be some sort of children's nativity presentation – that's non-negotiable. One thing you can be assured of with most churches is that there is activity in the nativity.

Of course, there's a price to be paid for this non-stop Christmas bustle. It's not just that you can find yourself staggering back to work almost with relief; it's that you haven't had time to think. We can be too busy to think what Christmas is about because we are too busy *doing* Christmas.

There's a curious Christmas tradition in several cities in Finland which goes back hundreds of years. It's called 'the Declaration of Christmas Peace'. At midday on Christmas Eve everyone gathers around the town hall to hear the mayor announce that as tomorrow will be 'the celebration of the birth of our Lord and Saviour' it is officially declared to be 'a time of peace'. The announcement comes with a solemn warning: 'Anybody who does not behave peacefully and quietly or behaves improperly shall be declared guilty and punished with a particular severity.'

Tempting as it is, legally enforcing a peaceful Christmas – especially with severe penalties – is probably not the way to go.

But it does make a point. This is a season when we should at some point put aside all distractions, pause, take a breath and think about what is really going on. So let me suggest one priority activity at Christmas. It is to *stop*. Put aside the wrapping paper, close the recipe book and instead find somewhere quiet to read the nativity story and reflect and pray.

In Luke's Gospel we read that the shepherds didn't just visit the holy family, they began talking about what they'd seen and heard and then they returned, glorifying and praising God for all the things they had heard and seen. In the middle of the account of this is a little phrase 'But Mary treasured up all these things and pondered them in her heart' (Luke 2:19). The mother of Jesus considered deeply what had happened and wondered about these events. It's not a bad principle.

One Christmas song that is not particularly well known but deserves to be is 'I wonder as I wander'. It's a folk hymn, written by American singer John Jacob Niles in the early part of the last century. There's a nice story about its origin. Niles was a folksong collector and when he was visiting a small town in the Appalachians in 1933, he came across a meeting with evangelical Christians. A small girl, dressed in little more than rags, sang a fragment of the song and Niles wrote it down and then later expanded it. Who originally composed the song remains unknown.

> I wonder as I wander out under the sky,
> How Jesus the Saviour did come for to die.
> For poor on'ry people like you and like I;
> I wonder as I wander out under the sky.

Incidentally, *on'ry* is probably best understood as Appalachian dialect for *ordinary*. It is an encouragement to wonder about Christmas.

Let me suggest two questions to ask yourself to help guide your thinking.

First, what does this mean? Do I understand what Christmas is all about? If you don't then read the Bible passages again.

Second, go further. Ask yourself the deeper, tougher question: 'What does this mean *for me?*' If you really understand what Christmas is about, will you let it change your life?

I wonder as I wander

I wonder as I wander out under the sky,
How Jesus the Saviour did come for to die
For poor on'ry people like you and like I;
I wonder as I wander out under the sky.

When Mary birthed Jesus 'twas in a cow's stall,
With wise men and farmers and shepherds and all.
But high from God's heaven, a star's light did fall,
And the promise of ages it then did recall.

If Jesus had wanted for any wee thing,
A star in the sky or a bird on the wing,
Or all of God's angels in heav'n for to sing,
He surely could have it, 'cause he was the King.

I wonder as I wander out under the sky,
How Jesus the Saviour did come for to die.
For poor on'ry people like you and like I;
I wonder as I wander out under the sky.

Day 14
THE ANGELS APPEAR TO THE SHEPHERDS

Angels get rather ignored these days. In the past, people used to wonder if there were unseen spiritual beings around them. These days, if we do wonder about anything invisible around us it is likely to be whether we have a decent 4G signal.

And yet . . . For one thing angels are present throughout the Bible. There are several hundred references to them and around half of these occur in the New Testament. Even authors like Luke, who was both a doctor and a historian, has no problem when it comes to talking about angels. Jesus himself referred to them frequently.

Not only that, it is probably true to say that the majority of people in the majority of the world in the majority of history have believed in or seen angels. And a surprising number of people turn out to have a story to tell about someone appearing at just the right time in their lives, and who in hindsight may well have been an angel.

There's a lot more that can be said about angels but here we just simply need to note that they occur in the Christmas story in the gospels of both Luke and Matthew. Given that angels seem to be closely involved with God's significant actions on earth it's hardly surprising that they make an appearance at the turning point of history, the birth of Jesus.

Not surprisingly, angels are widely celebrated in carols. Take, for instance, 'Angels from the realms of glory'.

> Angels, from the realms of glory,
> Wing your flight o'er all the earth;
> Ye who sang creation's story
> Now proclaim Messiah's birth:

It's worth making three observations about angels at this time of year.

Angels are witnesses. In the Bible, angels are God's messengers sent to proclaim some truth. So although on the human scale of things the birth of this particular baby might seem utterly insignificant, the appearance of angels makes the point that, despite appearances, this is a very important matter indeed. Caesar, Herod and Quirinius may think they are running the world but the angels are a reminder of where authority really lies.

Angels are warriors. Artists have misled us not simply in giving angels wings but in making them weak creatures. A common phenomenon in the Bible is that when angels reveal who they are, the universal reaction is awe and terror. Under God's authority they wield enormous power. In recording the appearance of the angels to the shepherds the Bible refers to them as 'a great company of the heavenly host'. Another translation (the New Living Translation) catches the force of the statement with 'the angel was joined by a vast host of others – the armies of heaven'. That's some *serious* power. As Maurice

Roberts has said, 'We rob ourselves of much joy if we forget the loving and caring presence all round about us of the angels of God.'

Angels are worshippers. Unlike us, who only see God in a distant way, angels see him perfectly. As a result they worship him perfectly. We may think that our worship is feeble and weak. Possibly true, but we are only one small voice in an enormous choir of praise.

It's worthwhile thinking about who angels are. Their role as witnesses, warriors and worshippers should be an encouragement to us. We, like them, should be a true *witness* to the truth of Christmas; it may be that we are also required to be *warriors* for what is good and right in the face of evil. Above all, we should join them in perfect *worship*.

Angels from the realms of glory

Angels, from the realms of glory,
Wing your flight o'er all the earth;
Ye who sang creation's story
Now proclaim Messiah's birth:

Refrain:
Come and worship, come and worship
Christ the newborn King
Come and worship, come and worship
Worship Christ, the newborn King.

Shepherds, in the field abiding,
Watching o'er your flocks by night,
God with man is now residing,
Yonder shines the Infant Light: *Refrain*

Sages, leave your contemplations,
Brighter visions beam afar;
Seek the great Desire of nations,
Ye have seen his natal star: *Refrain*

Sinners, wrung with true repentance,
Doomed for guilt to endless pains,
Justice now revokes the sentence,
Mercy calls you – break your chains: *Refrain*

Though an infant now we view him,
He shall fill his Father's throne,
Gather all the nations to him;
Every knee shall then bow down: *Refrain*

All creation, join in praising
God the Father, Spirit, Son,
Evermore your voices raising
To th'eternal Three in One: *Refrain*

Day 15
ADORATION OF
THE SHEPHERDS

Although monarchies are pretty much an endangered species in Western Europe, the birth of a royal child generates extraordinary interest. Even in countries that guillotined their royal family a long time ago, newsagents will be full of magazines with photo spreads of the infant and the smiling royal parents. Royal births have always been important. In the days when kings were properly kings, there was a great deal of anxiety about having an heir to the throne. Think of Henry VIII and those poor wives. Royal births should, by rights, be events that are celebrated by those in power and by the public.

One of the most significant aspects of Jesus' birth is the way that power is hidden in obscurity. Those in power are conspicuous by their absence when Jesus appears. That's perhaps surprising given the significance of this birth. Jesus is the long-awaited Deliverer coming to the Jewish people. And by long-awaited we mean *long*: he fulfils a promise given to David a thousand years earlier and one far, far older to Abraham.

By rights, this baby ought to have been born in Jerusalem, David's city, and it ought to have been in a palace. By rights, he should have been born with all the glory, comfort and majesty that human beings can devise, with numerous royal attendants and doctors. By rights, too, the infant should have been visited by the rulers, governors, high priests and all those in authority. By rights, there should have been royal proclamations, fireworks across the nation and celebratory cards from Caesar and other monarchs.

By rights . . . The fundamental point about the coming of Jesus to the world is that *rights* were put aside. As we all know, it was not like that. The birth at the first Christmas was in humility. The Son of God was born in poverty, in a space normally reserved for animals. There can be no doubt that Jesus was born into a setting that was about as poor and modest a place as we can imagine.

Given the situation it is perfectly appropriate that the first visitors were shepherds. Shepherds were useful people; after all, the sacrificial system just up the road in Jerusalem required vast numbers of sheep. Indeed it's a nice thought that they were guarding the sacrificial sheep, in which case their summons to the birth of the one who will be called 'the Lamb of God who takes away the sin of the world' is especially appropriate. Socially, however, shepherds were very much the bottom of the pile. Let's face it, while the sheep of any nativity play are clean, fluffy and dazzlingly white, sheep in the real world are off-colour, dirty and smelly. And, in those days, those who looked after them probably deserved the same adjectives.

Yet one of the tremendous things about the first Christmas is that God invites the shepherds as witnesses to the birth of the Messiah. The powerful, the rich, the lords and ladies of society – they all miss out. Instead, those at the bottom are invited in. The God of the Bible is someone who believes in inclusion. It's fascinating that what happens with the shepherds is exactly what Mary herself prophesied in the song that is traditionally called the *Magnificat*. One of the great themes of this is the way in which God will reverse the status of the world.

> He has brought down rulers from their thrones but has lifted up the humble. He has filled the hungry with good things but has sent the rich away empty. (Luke 1:52–53)

I'm sure this is an encouragement to many of us. We look around at the rich and the influential, those who portray themselves as the movers and makers of society and culture: the *really important* people, as they no doubt consider themselves. And most of us realise that we are not in that category and we never will be. If you feel excluded, be encouraged! God invites you to the birth of his Son. And if you consider yourself powerful and influential – be careful that you don't let your importance cause you to miss out on Christmas.

Shepherds get a mention in many carols. One in which they play a prominent part is 'See, amid the winter's snow'.

See, amid the winter's snow

See, amid the winter's snow,
Born for us on earth below,
See, the tender Lamb appears,
Promised from eternal years.

Refrain:
Hail, thou ever blessed morn!
Hail, redemption's happy dawn!
Sing through all Jerusalem,
'Christ is born in Bethlehem!'

Lo, within a manger lies
He who built the starry skies;
He who, throned in height sublime,
Sits among the cherubim. *Refrain*

Say, ye holy shepherds, say,
What your joyful news today?
Wherefore have ye left your sheep
On the lonely mountain steep? *Refrain*

'As we watched at dead of night,
Lo, we saw a wondrous light:
Angels singing "Peace On Earth"
Told us of the Saviour's birth.' *Refrain*

Sacred Infant, all divine,
What a tender love was thine,
Thus to come from highest bliss
Down to such a world as this. *Refrain*

Teach, O teach us, Holy Child,
By thy face so meek and mild,
Teach us to resemble thee,
In thy sweet humility. *Refrain*

Day 16
THE MAGI

By now, I suppose most people realise that the figures whom tradition has tended to call 'the Three Kings' or 'the Three Wise Men' are the result of some zealous embroidery over the years. The Bible simply talks about Magi – astrologers, prophets or, to play it safe, wise men – from somewhere to the east and it makes no mention of whether or not they were kings. Neither does it say anything about how many there were. And the idea that they were called Caspar, Melchior and Balthazar is about as intriguing as the names of Santa's reindeer. There are hints in the text that some time has passed since the birth of Jesus and the visit of the shepherds, so they aren't visiting a baby. It's perfectly possible that by now Jesus is a one- or two-year-old and it's an entertaining thought to imagine him amusing himself with the gifts in a toddler sort of way.

Even in their downgraded status as wise men the Magi are fascinating figures to appear in the Christmas story. We learn about the shepherds in Luke's Gospel and the Magi in Matthew's Gospel. Yet interestingly enough – and it's a phenomenon that occurs elsewhere in the Bible – two separate authors speak with a very similar voice. I made the point with the shepherds that these were people who were socially excluded and yet God in his grace summoned them to the infant Jesus. Superficially, the Magi seem totally different. Even if they weren't kings, they were able to afford gold, frankincense and myrrh, none of which came cheap.

The Magi have given rise to one of the most well-known of Christmas carols: 'We three kings of Orient are':

> We three kings of Orient are;
> Bearing gifts we traverse afar,
> Field and fountain, moor and mountain,
> Following yonder star.

The carol focuses on the three gifts – gold, myrrh and frankincense – and in the final verse it ties them in with the momentous idea that the infant in the manger is the one who is to be 'King and God and sacrifice'. Those are very important thoughts.

Nevertheless, here I simply want to point out something else. The fact is that these people were also outsiders. Not outsiders in the social or economic sense, but very definitely in terms of culture and religion. They were clearly not Jews. It's not just that they come from afar but they are practitioners in astrology, a subject that was considered an abomination by believing Jews. In fact, they come from such a distance that they are dangerously unaware of the reputation of the paranoid King Herod, whose habit of killing subjects, family members and even the occasional high priest had become almost routine. Despite the distance and the homicidal monarch, the Magi bring gifts and worship the child. Then, warned by God, they sensibly tiptoe away home by a back route, leaving Herod to have a monumental outburst and slaughter as many toddlers and babies in Bethlehem as he can find.

The Magi, then, are outsiders. And I find that encouraging. There are a lot of people who feel they don't fit in church. Maybe it's you who feels you are an outsider. Perhaps you don't speak English in a 'proper' way, perhaps you feel you come from the wrong culture or race. Actually, the church was designed from day one to be multicultural and multi-ethnic: if yours doesn't make you welcome, my advice is to find one that does.

But the point is that wherever you are from, God invites you to come and worship Jesus. Oh and don't worry, you don't need to bring gold, frankincense or myrrh – just bring yourself.

We three kings of Orient are

We three kings of Orient are;
Bearing gifts we traverse afar,
Field and fountain, moor and mountain,
Following yonder star.

O star of wonder, star of night,
Star with royal beauty bright,
Westward leading, still proceeding,
Guide us to thy perfect light.

CASPAR
Born a King on Bethlehem's plain
Gold I bring to crown him again,
King forever, ceasing never,
Over us all to reign. *Refrain*

MELCHIOR
Frankincense to offer have I;
Incense owns a Deity nigh;
Prayer and praising, voices raising,
Worshipping God on high. *Refrain*

BALTHAZAR

Myrrh is mine, its bitter perfume
Breathes a life of gathering gloom;
Sorrowing, sighing, bleeding, dying,
Sealed in the stone-cold tomb. *Refrain*

Glorious now behold him arise;
King and God and sacrifice;
Heav'n sings 'Alleluia',
'Alleluia' the earth replies. *Refrain*

Day 17
THE OPPOSITION TO THE BIRTH

In a world that is frequently mean, ugly and brutal, one of the attractions of popular representations of the nativity is the view of the Christmas season as a time of universal peace and goodwill. We may not expect niceness to endure during the year but we live in hope that at least it will persist during the Christmas season. Sadly, experience teaches us that in reality bad things happen at Christmas and hostilities between nations, communities and even within families can continue amid the tinsel and the turkey.

The Bible's account of Christmas is not one of a universal sunlit serene scene. With Herod's murderous attempt to eliminate the infant Jesus the darkest shadows fall over the picture. It's very easy to portray Herod as some sort of grotesque pantomime villain but unfortunately he is all too authentic to be a figure of fun. Anyone surveying modern history will be aware of the existence of people who, when threatened, are perfectly capable of ordering the massacre of a score of infants and writing it off as just one of those things you have to do. Whether for our own comfort or for that of children, we have tended to produce a sanitised, Disneyland Christmas not far removed from the local pantomime. The reality is that this is not a comfortable tale.

Buried under the artificial snow and Christmas lights is the tough story of a man taking his pregnant wife miles across country to register for tax purposes with an occupying power. Once at their destination our young couple find that there is not even a guestroom for them. The story echoes with so many uncomfortable and contemporary notes: oppression, taxation, occupation, humiliation. And that's before Herod goes into his murderous tantrum.

Christmas carols recognise the presence of good coming into the world and some make the point that the good is opposed. In fact, the hostility that Herod shows against the infant Jesus is not simply an expression of hatred against God and his Son by an evil man, but something stronger and deeper. The Bible's view of the way the world works is that there is a cosmic evil of demonic powers and authorities governed by an evil one who has set himself up against God. The first Christmas was an act of war. God sent his Deliverer into enemy territory and God's intervention into the world is an irritation to the devil. At the Incarnation, the cry from the devil was something along the lines of 'Why the hell can't he leave us alone?' Many Christmas carols recognise this; the one that is sometimes called the 'Coventry Carol', 'Lully, lullay, thou little tiny child' includes the chilling verse:

> Herod the king, in his raging,
> Chargèd he hath this day
> His men of might in his own sight
> All young children to slay.

And the carol 'Unto us a Child is born' includes the verse:

> Herod then with fear was filled:
> 'A prince,' he said, 'in Jewry!'
> All the little boys he killed
> At Bethl'em in his fury.

We may feel uncomfortable with the word *Jewry* and if it brings to mind the Holocaust and genocide then *uncomfortable* may be the right emotion. Evil still stalks the world.

'O little town of Bethlehem' has one of the most thought-provoking phrases in the entire canon of carols. Speaking of the first Christmas night and addressing the newborn Jesus we read, 'the hopes and fears of all the years are met in thee tonight'. For those that long for good, Jesus' birth is the focus of enormous hope. The Messiah has come! The Deliverer is here! Finally, evil is being challenged!

But for those who have sought evil, the nativity is a terrifying focus of fear. The arrival of the Christ child says to all tyrants, thugs and despots, 'Your days are numbered.' It's a delightful irony that the infant who was so homeless that he had nowhere to lay his head except in a manger is the one whose arrival serves notice of eviction from the world to the powers of evil.

The challenge posed by the Incarnation continues to the present day. Ultimately we are all forced into one of two choices: love him or hate him. Our lives ultimately must lead to him or away from him, to heaven or to hell. There is no neutral place. Do you want to love him or get rid of him?

Lully, lullay, thou little tiny child

(Coventry Carol)

Lully, lullay, thou little tiny child,
Bye bye, lully, lullay.
Lully, lullay, thou little tiny child,
Bye bye, lully, lullay.

O sisters too, how may we do
For to preserve this day
This poor youngling for whom we sing,
Bye bye, lully, lullay?

Herod the king, in his raging,
Chargèd he hath this day
His men of might in his own sight
All young children to slay.

That woe is me, poor child, for thee!
And ever mourn that day,
For thy parting not say nor sing,
Bye bye, lully, lullay.

Day 18
CHRIST THE KING

At Christmas there is always a risk of what could be called 'manger danger'. This is the tendency to focus on Jesus as the babe at Bethlehem – but I think to focus on that misses the point. One of the virtues of carols is that they look beyond the sweetness of the first Christmas to see its significance.

A theme that frequently emerges in carols is that of Jesus being *King*. In fact, one of the standard readings at Christmas time is from Isaiah chapter 9 and many of the verses there reverberate with the idea of kingship. Consider these two verses:

> For to us a child is born, to us a son is given, and the government will be on his shoulders. And he will be called Wonderful Counsellor, Mighty God, Everlasting Father, Prince of Peace. Of the greatness of his government and peace there will be no end. He will reign on David's throne

and over his kingdom, establishing and upholding it with justice and righteousness from that time on and for ever. (Isaiah 9:6–7)

Isaiah is prophesying that the child to come will be the one who will bear the weight of government, be the Prince of Peace and the one who will reign on David's throne and establish it for ever with justice and righteousness. This isn't exactly some over-imaginative interpretation of ambiguous verses: this is most definitely about a coming *King*. And not just a constitutional 21st-century monarch: a powerful mighty traditional KING with capital letters.

The other prophecy which is read at Christmas is Micah 5:2, 'But you, Bethlehem Ephrathah, though you are small among the clans of Judah, out of you will come for me one who will be ruler over Israel, whose origins are from of old, from ancient times.' Kingship again.

The idea that the baby is King in the biggest possible sense is actually everywhere in the accounts of the birth of Jesus. He is the Messiah, the one of the line of David, the *Lord*. The word

Messiah or *Christ* signifies the promised, God-appointed and God-anointed King. That Christ is King is a theme that continues throughout the gospels and is declared with tragic irony by the very non-Jewish governor Pontius Pilate in the placard he placed above the cross: 'This is the King of the Jews'.

Deep down, human beings like the idea of a king: someone who will reign and rule over a messy and corrupt world with justice and power; someone who will protect the weak and vulnerable against the proud and powerful. The problem is that our expectation is rarely matched by the reality. You can get sad kings who try to rule with justice but don't have the power to do so. And then you get bad kings who have the power but don't do justice. Indeed, because power corrupts, few powerful kings stay good. Jesus, however, is the King who is perfectly good and perfectly powerful.

One of the many Christmas carols that touches on this theme of Jesus as King is 'What child is this?'

What child is this, who, laid to rest
On Mary's lap is sleeping?

Whom angels greet with anthems sweet,
While shepherds watch are keeping?
This, this is Christ the King,
Whom shepherds guard and angels sing:
Haste, haste to bring him laud,
The Babe, the Son of Mary.

That Christ is King is a great idea but what does it actually mean? The fact is that the gospel accounts themselves give us some idea of what it means for Christ to be King. There we see, in the casting out of demons, the fact that he is King over every evil spiritual power. We see, as he stills storms and multiplies loaves and fishes, that he is King over nature. We see, as he heals the sick, that he is King over sickness and disease. We see, as he raises people from the grave, that he is King over death. We see, as he offers forgiveness, that he is King over sin. He is already King over everything.

The really big and provocative question is this: is he King over us? Does Jesus reign and rule over us?

What child is this?

What child is this, who, laid to rest
On Mary's lap is sleeping?
Whom angels greet with anthems sweet,
While shepherds watch are keeping?
This, this is Christ the King,
Whom shepherds guard and angels sing:
Haste, haste to bring him laud,
The Babe, the Son of Mary.

Why lies he in such mean estate,
Where ox and ass are feeding?
Good Christians, fear: for sinners here
The silent Word is pleading.
Nails, spear shall pierce him through,
The cross he bore for me, for you.
Hail, hail the Word made flesh,
The Babe, the Son of Mary.

So bring him incense, gold and myrrh,
Come, peasant, king, to own him.
The King of kings salvation brings,
Let loving hearts enthrone him.
Raise, raise the song on high,
The virgin sings her lullaby
Joy, joy for Christ is born,
The Babe, the Son of Mary.

Day 19

CHRISTMAS IS THE BEGINNING OF THE STORY OF JESUS

There is a story concerning the 19th-century poet and playwright Oscar Wilde that goes like this. As a student at Oxford, Wilde was asked in an oral exam to translate a passage from the Greek original of the New Testament. The passage chosen was from the trial of Jesus. An excellent linguist, Wilde translated the passage into English with speed and accuracy. The examiners, completely satisfied, told him that this was enough. Wilde, however, continued and it was only after some time that the examiners finally managed to persuade him to stop. 'Oh, do let me go on,' said Wilde, 'I want to see how it ends.'

The problem is that the story of Jesus is one that people have come to take for granted. They think that they know it. But do they? Do you? One of the important issues to do with the nativity is that it is not an ending, but a beginning. To seriously ask the question 'I want to see how it ends' is actually a very sensible one.

Jesus' birth at Bethlehem is just the beginning of the life of Christ and it's important. It's even more important that we don't just stop there. It's surely significant that two of the gospels, Mark and John, don't report the nativity story. They start straightaway with the life of Jesus. As we read the gospels we find that all the themes announced at Christmas recur and are expanded on.

We need to read the gospels and see the man that the infant became. We need to be challenged by Jesus' teaching and by his works of power. We need to be challenged by who Jesus claimed to be and above all by the cross. 'I want to see how it *ends*' is what Wilde is reported as saying but here lies the strangest thing of all. Every life on this earth comes to an end. Death writes the final page for every biography. But not this one. The story of Jesus continues.

One carol that includes this emphasis on the nativity being the beginning of the life of Jesus, the Son of God, is a modern carol, 'Mary did you know?'

> Mary, did you know that your baby boy will some day walk on water?
> Mary, did you know that your baby boy will save our sons and daughters?
> Did you know that your baby boy has come to make you new?
> This child that you've delivered, will soon deliver you.

There's a fascinating phrase right at the start of the Book of Acts which is the sequel to Luke's Gospel. Without any apology or warning, Luke writes what is one of the most unusual things ever written: 'In my former book, Theophilus, I wrote about all that Jesus *began* to do and to teach until the day he was taken up to heaven . . .' (Acts 1:1–2). Luke is saying that, despite Jesus' death, his story is far from over. He has been raised from the dead and he continues to live and act. Indeed, Christians believe that Jesus continues to work in the world today. The story of Jesus is one that doesn't end.

The really good news is that if we put our faith in Jesus *our* story doesn't end either. All those who are connected to him by faith have lives that will not end with the grave. This is not simply wishful thinking; it is based on the many promises that Jesus gives about an unending life. To take one verse from many, we read in John's Gospel that Jesus said, 'Very truly I tell you, whoever hears my word and believes him who sent me has eternal life and will not be judged but has crossed over from death to life' (John 5:24).

The story of the stable and the manger are the beginning of what Hollywood called – for once without exaggeration – *The Greatest Story Ever Told*. The story of Jesus continues throughout the world today and will continue for ever. His kingdom keeps going and, as it spreads, more and more people and nations are brought into it. The question we must all ask ourselves is this: have we been drawn into it? Have we accepted Christ and become part of the story that begins in Bethlehem but doesn't end. *Ever*.

Mary, did you know?

Mary, did you know that your baby boy will some day walk on water?
Mary, did you know that your baby boy will save our sons and daughters?
Did you know that your baby boy has come to make you new?
This child that you delivered, will soon deliver you.

Mary, did you know that your baby boy will give sight to a blind man?
Mary, did you know that your baby boy will calm the storm with his hand?
Did you know that your baby boy has walked where angels trod?
And when you kiss your little baby, you have kissed the face of God.

Oh Mary, did you know

The blind will see, the deaf will hear, the dead will live again.
The lame will leap, the dumb will speak the praises of the Lamb.

Mary, did you know that your baby boy is Lord of all creation?
Mary, did you know that your baby boy would one day rule the nations?
Did you know that your baby boy is heaven's perfect Lamb?
This sleeping child you're holding is the great I Am.

Day 20
CHRISTMAS LOOKS FORWARD TO EASTER

I mentioned at the start of these reflections the need for us to ask the question 'Why did Jesus come?' The answer I gave was that the human race needed a Redeemer. The idea of redemption – of having a life turned around for good – is never far from the surface at Christmas.

One of the classic and very seasonal tales of redemption is Charles Dickens' story *A Christmas Carol.* Most of us will have some idea of the story from the almost unlimited number of adaptations for TV, stage or screen. The central figure is that of the miser Scrooge. At the start of the story he is a cold, mean and greedy man without friends; he is both unloving and unlovable. One Christmas Eve he is visited by the ghost of a former business partner and then three successive ghosts: the Ghosts of Christmas Past, Christmas Present and Christmas Yet to Come. The shock of these visitors and what they reveal transforms him and he turns into the 'new Scrooge': a kindly, sociable man overflowing with generosity. It's a heart-warming story.

The gospel hinted at in the Christmas story is that a price must be paid to set people free. As we read on through the New Testament we realise that the price is a very high one indeed. It is no less than the death of Jesus, the Son of God, on the cross. The hints are already there in these first few chapters of Luke and Matthew. The baby will be called Jesus because he is going 'to save his people from their sins'. He who is going to be 'the Lamb of God who takes away the sin of the world' is born among animals and visited by shepherds. The Magi give him the gifts of gold, frankincense and myrrh. The last two are particularly significant: frankincense was used in worship as a fragrance associated with sacrifices; and myrrh is a spice used for embalming the dead. The shadow of the cross falls over the manger.

John 3:16 is one of the best-known verses in the Bible. The verse that follows it, however, is very relevant to Christmas. Let's take the two together:

> For God so loved the world that he gave his one and only Son, that whoever believes in him shall not perish but have eternal life. For God did not send his Son into the world to condemn the world, but to save the world through him. (John 3:16–17)

Jesus was sent into the world to save it: to give us salvation, to redeem us. One Christmas carol that keeps the cross firmly in focus is 'Christians, awake, salute the happy morn'. In the version from the *Lutheran Hymnal*, verse five reads:

> Oh, may we keep and ponder in our mind
> God's wondrous love in saving lost mankind!
> Trace we the Babe, who hath retrieved our loss,
> From his poor manger to his bitter cross,
> Tread in his steps, assisted by his grace,
> Till man's first heavenly state again takes place.

The idea here is that through the cross Jesus allows the human race to recover the fellowship with God that we had forfeited. Some churches have a tradition of using a real Christmas tree and then, after the festive season is over, of lopping off all the branches and turning it into a cross. There is a logic to that: the cradle and the cross are linked. The cradle leads to the cross.

For Christians the cross is no accidental tragedy, no unforeseen termination of an otherwise promising life. It is not a calamity but the culmination of Jesus' life and is in fact part of the plan of the Incarnation. The crucifixion is the act that the baby came into the world to suffer. John's Gospel records that the last thing Jesus uttered was 'It is finished'. The word used has the sense of 'It is completed', 'It is fulfilled' or even 'It is paid'. It's a little bit like someone finishing some wearisome task and announcing with relief and satisfaction, 'Job well done!'

What's the point of Christmas? The point is that it's the start of God's redemption of the human race. Jesus was born among us so that he might die for us. For me and for you.

Christians, awake, salute the happy morn

Christians, awake, salute the happy morn
Whereon the Saviour of the world was born.
Rise to adore the mystery of love,
Which hosts of angels chanted from above;
With them the joyful tidings first begun
Of God incarnate and the virgin's Son.

Then to the watchful shepherds it was told,
Who heard the angelic herald's voice: 'Behold,
I bring good tidings of a Saviour's birth
To you and all the nations upon earth;
This day hath God fulfilled his promised word;
This day is born a Saviour, Christ the Lord.'

He spake; and straightway the celestial choir
In hymns of joy, unknown before, conspire;
The praises of redeeming love they sang,
And heaven's whole orb with alleluias rang.
God's highest glory was their anthem still,
Peace upon earth and unto men goodwill.

To Bethlehem straight th'enlightened shepherds ran
To see the wonder God had wrought for man
And found, with Joseph and the blessed maid,
Her Son, the Saviour, in a manger laid;
Then to their flocks, still praising God, return.
And their glad hearts with holy rapture burn.

Oh, may we keep and ponder in our mind
God's wondrous love in saving lost mankind!
Trace we the Babe, who hath retrieved our loss,
From his poor manger to his bitter cross,
Tread in his steps, assisted by his grace,
Till man's first heavenly state again takes place.

Then may we hope, th'angelic hosts among,
To sing, redeemed, a glad triumphal song.
He that was born upon this joyful day
Around us all his glory shall display.
Saved by his love, incessant we shall sing
Eternal praise to heaven's almighty King.

Day 21
CHRISTMAS LOOKS FORWARD TO THE SECOND COMING

There are different types of logic. There is the logic of mathematics and philosophy but there is also what you might call the logic of drama or justice. Imagine, for instance, a story in which things are not as they seem. Perhaps there is a rich heroine disguised as a poor woman, or an innocent man falsely convicted of a serious crime, or even honourable people publicly shamed by things they have not done. The logic of justice or drama demands that, in the end, righteousness and truth triumph and justice is done. The masks are thrown away, the disguises are dropped and the world sees everything as it truly is. The sense we all seem to have that at some point falsehood and injustice must be overturned and reality must come into the open is a principle that goes far deeper than literature or drama.

For believers, the story of Jesus is of God himself, a being of inexpressible glory, awesome holiness and utter innocence, descending to become a human being. That would be awesome enough except that – almost unbelievably – he descends even further to become the very lowest kind of human: a man who begins his life in poverty and obscurity and ends it in agony and shame. The story of Jesus framed by the cradle and the cross demands that there is a final scene in which justice is done and the truth comes to the surface. Surely, he who became poor, guilty and shamed for us must be revealed to be who he really is: glorious, innocent and full of honour. The need for that final act is part of the reason for the Second Coming: an event which we can be certain lies ahead of us even if we cannot be certain of the time.

We need to hold on to this picture of Christ as the returning glorious King, finally and completely ending the long reign of evil. One of the problems with Christmas – the 'manger danger' – is that it focuses on the harmless, innocent, unthreatening baby, a scene that can arouse little more than affection and admiration. One of the problems with Easter is that we become preoccupied with Christ hanging helplessly on the cross, a scene that arouses compassion and pain. These images must be balanced by the promise of Christ's return in overwhelming majesty. It is good to think of Jesus as the baby in the manger and as the man hanging on the cross, but we must also look ahead to the third scene of the greatest drama in the universe: the revelation of the King in all his glory. From cradle, to cross, to crown.

With the belief in Christ's Second Coming comes the idea that much that seems so real and solid to us will vanish as quickly as the image on a computer screen disappears when we turn off the power. In its place will be a new, awesome reality of perfection and permanence in which everything we are and have done will be seen with utter clarity. The idea of Christ's return and his revelation in all his glory, and with it the destruction of all that is evil, is both alarming and reassuring.

'Once in royal David's city' mentions this tremendous truth. For the first few verses we sing about Christ coming in humility to Bethlehem. Then the carol shifts gear to a splendidly triumphant ending which deserves to be sung with great power.

Not in that poor lowly stable,
With the oxen standing by,
We shall see him; but in heaven,
Set at God's right hand on high;
Where like stars his children crowned
All in white shall wait around.

For those who have avoided Jesus all their lives, the idea that they will suddenly find they are on the wrong side of the King of the universe is a thought that is alarming and disturbing. Here, no wealth, no achievements, no worldly fame will be of any use. Alternatively, for those who have put their faith in Christ, the idea that they will finally be with their Saviour and King is extraordinarily reassuring and comforting. At his coming, they will be safe beyond all sorrow, sickness and sin; all that is wrong will be put right, all that has been lost will be found and all that is sad will be turned to joy. One of the oldest prayers recorded in the New Testament is a single word, *Maranatha*, which translated means 'Our Lord, come!' To which one can only add *Amen*.

Once in royal David's city

Once in royal David's city
Stood a lowly cattle shed,
Where a mother laid her baby
In a manger for his bed:
Mary was that mother mild,
Jesus Christ her little child.

He came down to earth from heaven,
Who is God and Lord of all,
And his shelter was a stable,
And his cradle was a stall;
With the poor, and mean, and lowly,
Lived on earth our Saviour holy.

And through all his wondrous childhood
He would honour and obey,
Love and watch the lowly maiden,
In whose gentle arms he lay:
Christian children all must be
Mild, obedient, good as he.

For he is our childhood's pattern;
Day by day, like us he grew;
He was little, weak and helpless,
Tears and smiles like us he knew;
And he feeleth for our sadness,
And he shareth in our gladness.

And our eyes at last shall see him,
Through his own redeeming love;
For that child so dear and gentle
Is our Lord in heaven above,
And he leads his children on
To the place where he is gone.

Not in that poor lowly stable,
With the oxen standing by,
We shall see him; but in heaven,
Set at God's right hand on high;
Where like stars his children crowned
All in white shall wait around.

Day 22
CHRISTMAS BRINGS HOPE

In the northern hemisphere and particularly in Britain, late December is the gloomiest of seasons. Daylight is at a minimum, temperatures are low and increasingly our winters seem to be dominated by an endless succession of rainstorms with few if any of the frosty sunlit days that can make winter a pleasure. To what extent Christmas was founded on a pagan festival at this time is a subject of great debate, but the fact that we are celebrating Christ's birth at this darkest of seasons is particularly appropriate. We need hope and encouragement. But where are we going to find it?

There are very few anthems for atheism – there's not a lot to sing about – but one of them is John Lennon's *Imagine*. It's all about imagining the absence of God and how wonderful things would be if he wasn't around.

In reality few thinking atheists can sing those optimistic words with genuine conviction. In fact, to pursue the idea of imagining that there is no God leads not to optimism but to despair. Imagine a world without Christmas, a world without any indication of God's intervention, a world with neither redemption nor hope: it's not exactly good news, is it? In fact, one of the first casualties of evicting God from the world is the very concept of hope. One of the great atheists of the 20th century was the philosopher Bertrand Russell and in his autobiography he wrote these words: 'There is darkness without, and when I die there will be darkness within. There is no splendour, no vastness anywhere, only triviality for a moment, and then nothing.' There are many issues with the view that is as despairing and devoid of hope as this. Not the least is the fact that hope is not simply a virtue that stands alone; it is a virtue that gives strength to everything else we do. Without hope, everything is an exercise in futility. In the absence of hope all we can do is shrug our shoulders and say, 'Why bother?'

Looking at the state of the world it seems that both atheists and Christians agree that we live in twilight. For the atheist, however, this is a twilight of evening that must sooner or later slip away into the darkest and most unending of nights. For the Christian, Christmas tells us that the twilight is merely the faint light that promises the dawn of an eternal day. That idea gives hope and strength to all that we do.

Appropriately, a number of carols sound a definitely upbeat note. One of these is 'Unto us a Boy is born' or 'Unto us a Child is born', in particular in verses four and five:

> Now may Mary's Son, who came
> So long ago to love us,
> Lead us all with hearts aflame
> Unto the joys above us.
>
> Omega and Alpha he!
> Let the organ thunder,
> While the choir with peals of glee
> Rends the air asunder.

Christmas changes everything. That God has committed himself to the world and the human race so deeply that he became one of us and has battled with evil is a thought that is capable of transforming the deadliest task and the dullest day. Bethlehem tells us that God cares about our world, about us and about what we do. Not only that but Christmas carries with it the promise that what was begun at Bethlehem in humility, will one day be completed in an eternal blaze of glory.

Unto us a Boy is born

(or Unto us a Child is born)

Unto us a Boy is born!
King of all creation:
Came he to a world forlorn,
The Lord of every nation.

Cradled in a stall was he
'Midst the cows and asses;
But the very beasts could see
That he all men surpasses.

Alternative second verse:
Christ, from heav'n descending low,
Comes on earth a stranger;
Ox and ass their Owner know
Now cradled in a manger.

Herod then with fear was filled:
'A prince,' he said, 'in Jewry!'
All the little boys he killed
At Bethl'em in his fury.

Now may Mary's Son, who came
So long ago to love us,
Lead us all with hearts aflame
Unto the joys above us.

Omega and Alpha he!
Let the organ thunder,
While the choir with peals of glee
Rends the air asunder.

Day 23
CHRISTMAS ENCOURAGES CONCERN FOR OTHERS

Christmas is all about God giving himself in Jesus to a world that didn't deserve him. It is the ultimate in grace: the greatest, costliest gift to the most needy and undeserving cause. It is about grace to the world in general and, if we are Christians, to you and me personally. And because we have received that grace, quite simply it should overflow from us. Because God gave us so much we should be those who want to give to others.

That's the principle. How does it work in practice? One carol that hints at how this works is 'It came upon the midnight clear'. It picks up two words present in the angels' message to the shepherds: peace and goodwill.

It came upon the midnight clear,
That glorious song of old,
From angels bending near the earth,
To touch their harps of gold:
'Peace on the earth, goodwill to men,
From heaven's all-gracious King' –
The world in solemn stillness lay
To hear the angels sing.

So for a starter think about *peace*. Think about your life. Are there broken relationships that you can mend? Is there anybody you need to show forgiveness to? Do you need to say sorry to someone? Is there a situation where you might possibly be able to be a peacemaker?

Then continue it with *goodwill.* Who is there around you that you can show kindness to? To some people Christmas is a celebration of all that they have, but for others it is a bitter reminder of all that they don't have. Consider the people you work with, talk to or are neighbours with. How can you do good to them this Christmas season?

It came upon the midnight clear

It came upon the midnight clear,
That glorious song of old,
From angels bending near the earth,
To touch their harps of gold:
'Peace on the earth, goodwill to men,
From heaven's all-gracious King' –
The world in solemn stillness lay
To hear the angels sing.

Still through the cloven skies they come
With peaceful wings unfurled,
And still their heavenly music floats
O'er all the weary world;
Above its sad and lowly plains
They bend on hovering wing,
And ever o'er its Babel-sounds
The blessed angels sing.

Yet with the woes of sin and strife
The world has suffered long;
Beneath the angel-strain have rolled
Two thousand years of wrong;
And man, at war with man, hears not
The love-song which they bring;
O hush the noise, ye men of strife,
And hear the angels sing!

And ye, beneath life's crushing load,
Whose forms are bending low,
Who toil along the climbing way
With painful steps and slow,
Look now! for glad and golden hours
Come swiftly on the wing.
Oh, rest beside the weary road
And hear the angels sing!

For lo! the days are hastening on
By prophet bards foretold,
When, with the ever-circling years
Comes round the age of gold;
When peace shall over all the earth
Its ancient splendours fling,
And the whole world give back the song
Which now the angels sing.

Day 24
BEING JOYFUL

As I have pointed out on a number of occasions in these reflections, our modern culture gets a lot wrong with Christmas. But one thing it gets right is that this should be a time for celebration. The gospel is *good* news – that's actually what the Greek word means – and Christmas is the beginning of the gospel and so it deserves celebration. In the Bible joy occurs in the Christmas story. So in Matthew we read that the Magi seeking to honour the new-born King Jesus were overcome with joy when they found him (Matthew 2:10). Millions of people since have been overcome by joy when they found Jesus. It was on 9th February 1975 when I received Christ into my life. In Luke's Gospel the angel tells the shepherds, 'Do not be afraid. I bring you good news that will cause great joy for all the people. Today in the town of David a Saviour has been born to you; he is the Messiah, the Lord' (Luke 2:10–11). That theme of joy continues through the New Testament. St Paul makes 131 references to joy in the ten letters attributed to him.

Christmas is indeed good news; it is in fact the best news imaginable. If you look at a newspaper or a news website, the sheer amount of evil and suffering can be utterly depressing. Christmas, however, brings a reminder that, in the end, good wins. In the first Christmas we see God making a promise that the days of evil are limited. In the baby Jesus we see God stepping forward into history and saying, 'This is my fight, I am on your side.'

For someone who believes in the truth of Christmas, *joy* is the appropriate response. Joy is not simply an emotion; true joy is a deep feeling that arises from truth and certainty. Joy is deeper, stronger and longer-lasting than either cheerfulness or happiness. Quite often joy is a triumph of faith over feelings. People can experience joy in prison and in poverty. Joy is so important and powerful that it spills over into everything else. Not only is it impossible to hide, but people who feel joyful have to express why they feel it and the reasons for it. No one who has joy because of their relationship to Christ can be anything other than an effective witness – they can't help talking to other people about him.

A key thing here is to realise that Christmas is not simply a historical event of long ago (which it is), nor an event that has implications for the world (which it is), but an event which has a personal significance. It should mean something for you and me. We have seen the wise men and the shepherds summoned to gather round the infant Jesus. I want to suggest that this summons applies to all. There is joy to be found around the cradle. But you have to come and receive it. God wants to give us the gift of his Holy Spirit, which gives us Christ's peace and presence and produces joy.

It's not uncommon at carol services to hear someone rather grumpily mumble something along the lines of, 'They wrote *proper* songs then. None of this modern nonsense . . .' Actually, they did write nonsense then too, it's just that over the years congregations have put the nonsense ones in the bin. And they do write good songs today. One that is worth knowing, is from Keith Getty and Stuart Townend. I want to mention it not simply because it talks about joy but because it brings in so many of the themes of Christmas: it's all there in just four verses.

Joy has dawned upon the world

Joy has dawned upon the world,
Promised from creation –
God's salvation now unfurled,
Hope for ev'ry nation.
Not with fanfares from above,
Not with scenes of glory,
But a humble gift of love –
Jesus born of Mary.

Sounds of wonder fill the sky
With the songs of angels
As the mighty Prince of Life
Shelters in a stable.
Hands that set each star in place,
Shaped the earth in darkness,
Cling now to a mother's breast,
Vuln'rable and helpless.

Shepherds bow before the Lamb,
Gazing at the glory;
Gifts of men from distant lands
Prophesy the story.
Gold – a King is born today,
Incense – God is with us,
Myrrh – his death will make a way,
And by his blood he'll win us.

Son of Adam, Son of heaven,
Given as a ransom;
Reconciling God and man,
Christ, our mighty champion!
What a Saviour! What a Friend!
What a glorious myst'ry!
Once a babe in Bethlehem,
Now the Lord of hist'ry.

Day 25

CHRISTMAS IS AN EVENT THAT DEMANDS OUR COMMITMENT

Apparently there are over 7.5 billion people on the planet. That's a lot of people. It can feel slightly intimidating to realise that you are just one in seven-and-a-half billion. That sense of insignificance can be made worse by the increasingly anonymous and digital world that we live in. We are addressed by robots on the phone, are known to banks by account numbers, are identified at airports by biometric data. The question that many of us think about is this: Am *I* worth anything? Do *I* matter?

It's worth remembering as we conclude our advent Christmas reflections that God could have ensured that the account of how he intervened in the world was written in purely abstract, theological or philosophical terms. Instead he gives it to us as a story. I find that very helpful. Although they are only sketched out in the Bible we can – and do – fill in the characters involved. So we can imagine Mary as the slightly flustered teenage mother, see Joseph as the bewildered father rendered awkward by events, visualise the shepherds as rough-and-ready rustics, and conjure up the Magi with their exotic glamour. One of the virtues of nativity plays, however badly done, is that they reinforce this sense that this is an event that involves real people.

This is invaluable. Despite the unrelenting efforts of governments, banks, supermarkets and local authorities, you and I remain human beings. We are not simply barcodes, demographic units, Social Security numbers or any other kind of dehumanising digital code. We are *people*. And the very existence of Mary, Joseph, the shepherds and the entire cast of the nativity make the point that *people* count. God, the Person who made us all people in his image, doesn't save people *en masse* as if they were parts of some anonymous quota system; he saves individual people like you and me.

We all need to realise this: God cares for us as persons and he cares for you. He cares for who you are, with your name, your history, your character and your problems. The Christmas message is not some mass posting to the whole of humanity with the greeting 'To whom it may concern'; it is a message for you. *Personally*.

This is the season when we get all the corporate Christmas cards with our name inserted by computer. We glance at them and then put them on the bookshelf with no further thought; we know they are valueless. The Christmas message from God to you is nothing like this. Consider it as a carefully handwritten note, addressed to you personally and signed by God himself. You can imagine that it reads, 'Jesus Christ, Redeemer of the world, invites you to attend his birth and give him your worship.' This Christmas you are given something that is, in every sense, a *personal* invitation.

One of the very greatest Christmas carols is 'O little town of Bethlehem'. It ends with the following verse:

O holy Child of Bethlehem,
Descend to us, we pray.
Cast out our sin and enter in;
Be born in us today.
We hear the Christmas angels
The great glad tidings tell;
O come to us, abide with us,
Our Lord, Emmanuel.

I encourage you to personalise it and pray it is as a prayer:

O holy Child of Bethlehem,
Descend to *me*, *I* pray.
Cast out *my* sin and enter in;
Be born in *me* today.
I hear the Christmas angels
The great glad tidings tell;
O come to *me*, abide with me,
My Lord, Emmanuel.

Make it your prayer. And let God answer it.

O little town of Bethlehem

O little town of Bethlehem,
How still we see thee lie!
Above thy deep and dreamless sleep
The silent stars go by.
Yet in thy dark streets shineth
The everlasting Light;
The hopes and fears of all the years
Are met in thee tonight.

For Christ is born of Mary,
And gathered all above,
While mortals sleep, the angels keep
Their watch of wondering love.
O morning stars, together
Proclaim the holy birth,
And praises sing to God the King,
And peace to all on earth.

How silently, how silently
The wondrous gift is given!
So God imparts to human hearts
The blessings of his heaven.
No ear may hear his coming,
But in this world of sin,
Where meek souls will receive him, still
The dear Christ enters in.

O holy Child of Bethlehem,
Descend to us, we pray.
Cast out our sin and enter in;
Be born in us today.
We hear the Christmas angels
The great glad tidings tell;
O come to us, abide with us,
Our Lord, Emmanuel.

Reference

Day 1
Joy to the world!
Written by Isaac Watts.
First published in 1719.

Day 2
On Christmas night all Christians sing
(Sussex Carol)
Traditional. First published in 1684.

Day 3
God rest you merry, gentlemen
Traditional. First published c.1760.

Day 4
O come, O come, Emmanuel
From the Latin *Veni, veni, Emmanuel*
(13th century).

Day 5
While shepherds watched
Written by Nahum Tate c.1700.

Day 6
The angel Gabriel from heaven came
(Gabriel's Message)
Translation by Sabine Baring-Gould.
Current version dates from the 1890s.

Day 7
A virgin most pure
Author unknown c.1660.

Day 8
Away in a manger
The first two verses were published in
1884, author unknown. Third verse by
J.T. McFarland published in 1892.

Day 9
[1] The Nicene Creed states 'Light of Light,
very God of very God, begotten,
not made, being of one substance
with the Father'.
O come, all ye faithful
From the Latin *Adeste Fideles* c.1751.

Day 10
In the bleak midwinter
Written by Christina Rossetti in 1872.

Day 11
See him lying on a bed of straw
(Calypso Carol)
Written by Michael Perry.
Copyright © Mrs B. Perry, administered by
The Jubilate Group, copyrightmanager@
jubilate.co.uk. Used by permission.

Day 12
Hark! the herald angels sing
Written by Charles Wesley and
George Whitfield. First published in 1739.

Day 13
I wonder as I wander
Written by John Jacob Niles.
Copyright © 1934 G. Schirmer Inc.
All rights reserved. International copyright
secured. Used by permission of Chester
Music Limited trading as G. Schirmer.

Day 14
Angels from the realms of glory
Written by James Montgomery c.1816.

Day 15
See, amid the winter's snow
Written by Edward Caswall.
First published in 1871.

Day 16
We three kings of Orient are
Written by John Henry Hopkins in 1857.

Day 17
Lully, lullay, thou little tiny child
(Coventry Carol)
Traditional (15th century).

Day 18
What child is this?
Written by William Chatterton Dix in 1865.

Day 19
Mary, did you know?
Written by Mark Lowry and Buddy
Greene. Copyright © 1991, 1993 Rufus
Music (Adm. by Capitol CMG Publishing) /
Word Music (www.songsolutions.org).
Used by permission.

Day 20
**Christians, awake, salute the
happy morn**
Written by John Byrom in 1745.

Day 21
Once in royal David's city
Written by Cecil Frances Alexander.
First published in 1848.

Day 22
Unto us a Boy is born
(or Unto us a Child is born)
Traditional (14th century).

It came upon the midnight clear
Written by Edmund Sears.
First published in 1849.

Joy has dawned upon the world
Written by Keith Getty and Stuart
Townend. Copyright © 2004 Thankyou
Music (Adm. by Capitol CMG Publishing
excl. UK and Europe, adm. by Integrity
Music, part of the David C. Cook family,
songs@integritymusic.com). Used by
permission.

O little town of Bethlehem
Written by Phillips Brooks in 1868.